Better Homes and Gardens.

Pasta

Easy Everyday Recipe Library

BETTER HOMES AND GARDENS® BOOKS

Des Moines, Iowa

EASY EVERYDAY RECIPE LIBRARY
Better Homes and Gardens® Books, An imprint of Meredith® Books
Published for Creative World Enterprises LP, West Chester, Pennsylvania
www.creativeworldcooking.com

Pasta
Project Editors: Spectrum Communication Services, Inc.
Project Designers: Seif Visual Communications
Copy Chief: Catherine Hamrick
Copy and Production Editor: Terri Fredrickson
Contributing Proofreaders: Kathy Eastman, Susan J. Kling
Electronic Production Coordinator: Paula Forest
Editorial and Design Assistants: Judy Bailey, Mary Lee Gavin, Karen Schirm
Test Kitchen Director: Lynn Blanchard
Production Director: Douglas M. Johnston
Production Managers: Pam Kvitne, Marjorie J. Schenkelberg

Meredith® Books
Editor in Chief: James D. Blume
Design Director: Matt Strelecki
Managing Editor: Gregory H. Kayko

Director, Sales & Marketing, Retail: Michael A. Peterson
Director, Sales & Marketing, Special Markets: Rita McMullen
Director, Sales & Marketing, Home & Garden Center Channel: Ray Wolf
Director, Operations: George A. Susral

Vice President, General Manager: Jamie L. Martin

Better Homes and Gardens® Magazine
Editor in Chief: Jean LemMon
Executive Food Editor: Nancy Byal

Meredith Publishing Group
President, Publishing Group: Christopher M. Little
Vice President, Consumer Marketing & Development: Hal Oringer

Meredith Corporation
Chairman and Chief Executive Officer: William T. Kerr

Chairman of the Executive Committee: E. T. Meredith III

Creative World Enterprises LP
Publisher: Richard J. Petrone
Design Consultants to Creative World Enterprises: Coastline Studios, Orlando, Florida

All of us at Better Homes and Gardens® Books are dedicated to providing you with the information and ideas you need to create delicious foods. We welcome your comments and suggestions. Write to us at: Better Homes and Gardens Books, Cookbook Editorial Department, 1716 Locust St., Des Moines, Iowa 50309-3023.

Our seal assures you that every recipe in *Pasta* has been tested in the Better Homes and Gardens® Test Kitchen. This means that each recipe is practical and reliable, and meets our high standards of taste appeal. We guarantee your satisfaction with this book for as long as you own it.

Cover photo: Pasta Rosa-Verde
(see recipe, page 42)

Dress it up or play it down. Pasta offers endless
possibilities for a fine dining experience, a quick
family supper, and every meal in-between.
What other food combines so deliciously with beef, pork,
chicken, and seafood, not to mention many vegetables?
And the sauces are just as varied—rich cream sauces,
spicy tomato sauces, and garlicky butter sauces.

To enjoy the versatile good taste of pasta, simply
turn the pages and choose a dish that fills
the bill for dinner tonight.

CONTENTS

Chili Macaroni

Wagon wheel macaroni and green beans replace the kidney beans in this chili-style dish.

12	ounces ground beef or ground raw turkey
1	medium onion, chopped (½ cup)
1	14½-ounce can Mexican-style stewed tomatoes
1¼	cups tomato juice
2	tablespoons canned diced green chili peppers, drained
2	teaspoons chili powder
½	teaspoon garlic salt
1	cup packaged dried wagon wheel macaroni or elbow macaroni
1	cup loose-pack frozen cut green beans
1	cup shredded cheddar cheese (4 ounces)

In a large skillet cook ground beef or turkey and onion till meat is brown. Drain fat.

Stir stewed tomatoes, tomato juice, chili peppers, chili powder, and garlic salt into the meat mixture. Bring to boiling. Stir in pasta and green beans. Return to boiling; reduce heat. Cover and simmer about 15 minutes or till pasta and beans are tender.

To serve, spoon into bowls. Sprinkle each serving with shredded cheddar cheese. Makes 4 servings.

Nutrition information per serving: 427 calories, 29 g protein, 32 g carbohydrate, 21 g fat (10 g saturated), 83 mg cholesterol, 1,118 mg sodium.

Selecting Ground Beef

For lower-fat cooking, choose the leanest ground beef possible. Ground beef can range in fat from 75 percent lean (25 percent fat) to 97 percent lean (3 percent fat). For soups, stews, tacos, or casseroles, use 95 to 97 percent lean ground beef. Because very lean ground beef tends to crumble and be less juicy, you may want to use ground beef with slightly more fat for meat loaves, burgers, and meatballs.

Stovetop Stroganoff

You need only one skillet for this take-off on classic stroganoff.

12 ounces beef tenderloin steak or beef sirloin steak
1 tablespoon margarine or butter
1½ cups sliced fresh mushrooms
1 medium onion, cut into thin wedges
1 clove garlic, minced
2 cups water
4 ounces packaged dried mafalda or fettuccine, broken
2 teaspoons instant beef bouillon granules
¼ teaspoon pepper
1 8-ounce carton dairy sour cream or plain yogurt
2 tablespoons all-purpose flour
1 tablespoon snipped parsley

Trim fat from meat. Partially freeze meat. Thinly slice meat across the grain into bite-size strips.

In a large skillet cook and stir the meat in margarine or butter till meat is brown. Remove meat from skillet.

Add mushrooms, onion, and garlic to skillet. Cook and stir till vegetables are tender. Stir in the water, pasta, bouillon granules, and pepper. Bring to boiling; reduce heat. Cover and simmer about 12 minutes or till pasta is tender, stirring frequently.

Meanwhile, stir together sour cream or yogurt and flour. Stir sour cream mixture and parsley into the pasta mixture. Return meat strips to the skillet. Cook till bubbly, stirring gently. Cook and stir for 1 minute more. Makes 4 servings.

Nutrition information per serving: 408 calories, 23 g protein, 31 g carbohydrate, 21 g fat (10 g saturated), 73 mg cholesterol, 539 mg sodium.

Baked Mostaccioli with Meat Sauce

Bake these single-serving casseroles, topped with lots of melted cheese, for a hot and satisfying supper.

8 ounces packaged dried mostaccioli or cavatelli

1 14½-ounce can whole Italian-style tomatoes

½ of a 6-ounce can (⅓ cup) tomato paste

¼ cup dry red wine or water

½ teaspoon sugar

½ teaspoon dried oregano, crushed

½ teaspoon dried thyme, crushed

¼ teaspoon pepper

1 pound ground beef

1 medium onion, chopped (½ cup)

1 clove garlic, minced

½ cup sliced pimiento-stuffed green olives

1 cup shredded mozzarella cheese (4 ounces)

Cook pasta according to package directions. Drain pasta; rinse with cold water. Drain again. In a blender container or food processor bowl combine undrained tomatoes, tomato paste, wine or water, sugar, oregano, thyme, and pepper. Cover and blend or process till smooth. Set aside.

In a large skillet cook ground beef, onion, and garlic till meat is brown. Drain fat. Stir in the tomato mixture. Bring to boiling; reduce heat. Cover and simmer for 10 minutes. Stir in pasta and olives.

Divide mixture among six 10-ounce casseroles. Bake in a 375° oven for 15 minutes. (Or, spoon into a 2-quart casserole and bake for 30 minutes.) Sprinkle with the mozzarella cheese. Bake about 5 minutes more or till heated through. Makes 6 servings.

Nutrition information per serving: 367 calories, 25 g protein, 38 g carbohydrate, 13 g fat (5 g saturated), 58 mg cholesterol, 572 mg sodium.

Pasta Pizza

This hybrid recipe arranges favorite casserole ingredients to create an outstanding dish that looks and tastes like pizza.

5   ounces packaged dried corkscrew
    macaroni (2 cups)
1   beaten egg
¼   cup milk
2   tablespoons grated Parmesan cheese
8   ounces ground beef
1   small onion, chopped (⅓ cup)
1   clove garlic, minced
1   14½-ounce can Italian-style stewed
    tomatoes
1   cup green and/or yellow sweet
    pepper cut into 2-inch strips
½   teaspoon dried Italian seasoning,
    crushed
1   4½-ounce jar sliced mushrooms,
    drained
¼   teaspoon crushed red pepper
1   cup shredded mozzarella cheese
    (4 ounces)

Cook pasta according to package directions. Drain pasta; rinse with cold water. Drain again.

For pasta crust, in a large mixing bowl combine egg, milk, and Parmesan cheese. Stir in pasta. Spread pasta mixture evenly in a greased 12-inch pizza pan. Bake in a 350° oven for 20 minutes.

Meanwhile, in a large skillet cook ground beef, onion, and garlic till meat is brown. Drain fat. Add undrained tomatoes (cut up any large pieces of tomato), pepper strips, and Italian seasoning to meat mixture. Bring to boiling; reduce heat. Simmer, uncovered, for 10 to 12 minutes or till pepper strips are crisp-tender and most of the liquid is evaporated, stirring once or twice. Stir in mushrooms and crushed red pepper.

Spoon meat mixture over pasta crust. Sprinkle with mozzarella cheese. Bake for 10 to 12 minutes more or till heated through and cheese is melted. To serve, cut into wedges. Makes 6 servings.

Nutrition information per serving: 259 calories, 18 g protein, 27 g carbohydrate, 9 g fat (4 g saturated), 72 mg cholesterol, 479 mg sodium.

Taco Spaghetti

Feel like Mexican cuisine tonight? This tasty combination captures south-of-the-border flavors.

5 ounces packaged dried spaghetti, linguine, or fettuccine, broken
1 pound ground beef or ground raw turkey
1 large onion, chopped (1 cup)
¾ cup water
½ of a 1¼-ounce envelope (2 tablespoons) taco seasoning mix
1 11-ounce can whole kernel corn with sweet peppers, drained
1 cup sliced pitted ripe olives
1 cup shredded Cojack or cheddar cheese (4 ounces)
½ cup salsa
1 4-ounce can diced green chili peppers, drained
6 cups shredded lettuce
1 cup broken tortilla chips
1 medium tomato, cut into wedges
Dairy sour cream (optional)

Cook pasta according to package directions. Drain pasta; rinse with cold water. Drain again.

In a 12-inch skillet cook ground beef or turkey and onion till meat is brown. Drain fat. Stir in water and taco seasoning. Bring to boiling; reduce heat. Simmer, uncovered, for 2 minutes, stirring occasionally. Stir in cooked pasta, corn, olives, half of the shredded cheese, the salsa, and chili peppers.

Transfer mixture to a lightly greased 2-quart round casserole. Cover and bake in a 350° oven for 15 to 20 minutes or till heated through. Sprinkle with the remaining cheese.

Serve with lettuce, tortilla chips, and tomato wedges. If desired, top with sour cream. Makes 6 servings.

Nutrition information per serving: 438 calories, 26 g protein, 42 g carbohydrate, 21 g fat (8 g saturated), 66 mg cholesterol, 949 mg sodium.

Beef Strips with Vermicelli

Strips of top round steak make a lean choice for this sauce whether you are counting calories or pennies.

8   ounces boneless beef top round
    steak
4   ounces packaged dried vermicelli
    or spaghetti
1   tablespoon cooking oil
1   medium onion, chopped (½ cup)
1   14½-ounce can tomato wedges
1   9-ounce package frozen Italian-style
    green beans or cut green beans
1   4-ounce can sliced mushrooms,
    drained
½   of a 6-ounce can (⅓ cup) Italian-
    style tomato paste
½   teaspoon fennel seed, crushed
    (optional)
¼   teaspoon pepper
1   tablespoon grated Parmesan cheese
    Grated Parmesan cheese (optional)

Trim fat from meat. Partially freeze meat. Thinly slice meat across the grain into bite-size strips. Cook pasta according to package directions. Drain; keep warm.

Meanwhile, for sauce, in a large skillet heat oil over medium-high heat. Add meat and onion. Stir-fry for 2 to 3 minutes or till meat is brown.

Stir in undrained tomatoes, green beans, mushrooms, tomato paste, fennel seed (if desired), and pepper. Bring to boiling; reduce heat. Simmer, uncovered, for 7 to 8 minutes or till slightly thickened, stirring frequently. Stir in the 1 tablespoon Parmesan cheese.

Arrange pasta on individual plates or a large platter. Spoon the sauce over pasta. If desired, sprinkle with additional Parmesan cheese. Makes 4 servings.

Nutrition information per serving: 278 calories, 18 g protein, 38 g carbohydrate, 7 g fat (2 g saturated), 28 mg cholesterol, 488 mg sodium.

Fusilli with Creamy Tomato And Meat Sauce

Whipping cream enriches this herbed tomato and meat sauce. Serve it over your favorite pasta strands.

12 ounces ground beef or ground raw turkey
1 large onion, chopped (1 cup)
2 cloves garlic, minced
2 14-ounce cans peeled Italian-style tomatoes, cut up
1 teaspoon dried Italian seasoning, crushed
½ teaspoon sugar
¼ teaspoon salt
⅛ teaspoon pepper
8 ounces packaged dried fusilli, vermicelli, or spaghetti
½ cup whipping cream
2 tablespoons snipped parsley
 Fresh rosemary sprigs (optional)

For sauce, in a large saucepan cook beef or turkey, onion, and garlic till meat is brown. Drain fat. Stir in the undrained tomatoes, Italian seasoning, sugar, salt, and pepper. Bring to boiling; reduce heat. Simmer, uncovered, about 40 minutes or till most of liquid has evaporated, stirring occasionally.

Meanwhile, cook the pasta according to package directions. Drain; keep warm.

Gradually stir the whipping cream into the sauce. Heat through, stirring constantly. Remove from heat. Stir in parsley.

Arrange the pasta on individual plates or a large platter. Spoon the sauce over the pasta. If desired, garnish with fresh rosemary sprigs. Makes 4 servings.

Nutrition information per serving: 523 calories, 26 g protein, 59 g carbohydrate, 21 g fat (10 g saturated), 94 mg cholesterol, 534 mg sodium.

Piping Hot Pasta

To keep pasta warm, return the hot drained pasta to the hot cooking pan and cover it. To avoid overcooking the pasta and to prevent sticking, hold it no longer than 10 minutes and stir it once or twice.

Bow Ties with Sausage & Peppers

You will be amazed that so few ingredients generate so much flavor. For a lower-fat version, use Italian-style ground turkey sausage.

8 ounces packaged dried large bow-tie pasta
12 ounces spicy Italian sausage links
2 medium red sweet peppers, cut into ¾-inch pieces
½ cup vegetable broth or beef broth
¼ teaspoon coarsely ground black pepper
¼ cup snipped Italian parsley

Cook pasta according to package directions. Drain; keep warm.

Meanwhile, cut the sausage into 1-inch pieces. In a large skillet cook sausage and sweet peppers over medium-high heat till sausage is brown. Drain fat.

Stir the vegetable or beef broth and black pepper into sausage mixture. Bring to boiling; reduce heat. Simmer, uncovered, for 5 minutes. Remove from heat. Pour the sausage mixture over pasta; add parsley. Toss gently to coat. Makes 4 servings.

Nutrition information per serving: 397 calories, 24 g protein, 38 g carbohydrate, 18 g fat (6 g saturated), 94 mg cholesterol, 713 mg sodium.

Snipping Savvy

Snipping parsley and other fresh herbs takes only a few moments. Loosely pack the cleaned and dried leaves in a glass measuring cup. Use kitchen shears to cut them into small uniform pieces. This method eliminates the work of washing a cutting board.

Sausage, Broccoli, and Pasta Toss

No time to cook? Here's a quick-and-easy supper dish to serve in a pinch.

1 cup packaged dried tricolor or plain tortellini (about ½ of a 7-ounce package)
3 cups broccoli flowerets
8 ounces fully cooked smoked Polish sausage, halved lengthwise and thinly bias-sliced
1 tablespoon margarine or butter
1 tablespoon all-purpose flour
1 teaspoon caraway seed
1 cup milk
1 cup shredded process Swiss cheese (4 ounces)
1 tablespoon coarse-grain brown mustard

In a Dutch oven or large saucepan cook tortellini in a large amount of boiling salted water for 10 minutes, stirring occasionally. Add broccoli and sausage. Return to boiling and cook about 5 minutes more or till pasta is tender but slightly firm and broccoli is crisp-tender, stirring occasionally. Drain; keep warm.

Meanwhile, in a medium saucepan melt margarine or butter. Stir in flour and caraway seed. Add milk all at once. Cook and stir till thickened and bubbly. Add cheese and mustard, stirring till cheese melts. Pour over tortellini mixture; toss to coat. Makes 4 servings.

Nutrition information per serving: 482 calories, 26 g protein, 25 g carbohydrate, 31 g fat (12 g saturated), 70 mg cholesterol, 925 mg sodium.

Cheesy Ham and Linguine

Make dinner easy on yourself. Buy the cut-up vegetables from your grocery store's salad bar.

6 ounces packaged dried spinach and/or plain linguine
2 medium carrots, cut into ½-inch pieces (1 cup)
1 cup broccoli flowerets
1 cup sliced fresh mushrooms
2 tablespoons margarine or butter
2 tablespoons all-purpose flour
1 tablespoon snipped parsley
½ teaspoon dried basil, crushed
1¼ cups milk
6 ounces sliced fully cooked ham, cut into bite-size strips
½ cup shredded cheddar cheese

In a Dutch oven or large saucepan cook pasta and carrots in a large amount of boiling salted water for 7 minutes, stirring occasionally. Add broccoli. Return to boiling and cook for 3 to 5 minutes more or till pasta is tender but slightly firm and vegetables are crisp-tender. Drain; keep warm.

Meanwhile, cook mushrooms in margarine or butter till tender. Stir in flour, parsley, and basil. Add milk all at once. Cook and stir till thickened and bubbly. Add ham and cheese, stirring till cheese melts. Pour over pasta and vegetables; toss to coat. Makes 4 servings.

Nutrition information per serving: 417 calories, 23 g protein, 47 g carbohydrate, 15 g fat (6 g saturated), 33 mg cholesterol, 711 mg sodium.

Ham and Macaroni Salad

Chock full of ham and Monterey Jack cheese, this cool and creamy salad is perfect for a potluck picnic.

1 cup packaged dried wagon wheel or elbow macaroni
1½ cups cubed fully cooked ham (8 ounces)
4 ounces Monterey Jack or cheddar cheese, cut into cubes (1 cup)
1 cup frozen peas
1 stalk celery, thinly sliced (½ cup)
¼ cup finely chopped onion
2 tablespoons diced pimiento
½ cup mayonnaise or salad dressing
¼ cup sweet pickle relish or chopped sweet pickle
Dash pepper
1 to 2 tablespoons milk (optional)
8 cherry tomatoes, halved
Fresh parsley sprig (optional)

Cook pasta according to package directions. Drain pasta; rinse with cold water. Drain again.

In a large mixing bowl combine pasta, ham, cheese, peas, celery, onion, and pimiento. Toss gently to mix.

For dressing, in a small mixing bowl stir together mayonnaise or salad dressing, pickle relish or chopped pickle, and pepper. Pour dressing over pasta mixture. Toss to coat. Cover and chill for 4 to 24 hours.

Just before serving, stir in milk, if necessary. Spoon pasta mixture into a serving bowl. Arrange cherry tomato halves around edge of bowl. If desired, garnish with parsley. Makes 4 servings.

Nutrition information per serving: 534 calories, 25 g protein, 32 g carbohydrate, 34 g fat (10 g saturated), 71 mg cholesterol, 1,175 mg sodium.

Spaghetti and Sausage Pie

Good recipes never go away. Year after year, this perennial favorite keeps popping up in our test kitchen.

5 ounces packaged dried spaghetti
1 beaten egg
⅓ cup grated Parmesan cheese
1 tablespoon margarine or butter,
      cut up
1 beaten egg
1 cup cream-style cottage cheese,
      drained
⅛ teaspoon pepper
8 ounces bulk pork sausage, Italian
      sausage, or bulk turkey sausage
1 cup sliced fresh mushrooms
1 medium onion, chopped (½ cup)
¼ cup chopped green sweet pepper
1 8-ounce can pizza sauce
½ cup shredded mozzarella cheese
      (2 ounces)

Cook spaghetti according to package directions. Drain spaghetti; rinse with cold water. Drain again.

For spaghetti crust, in a medium mixing bowl combine 1 egg, Parmesan cheese, and margarine or butter. Add spaghetti; toss to coat. Press the spaghetti mixture against the bottom and side of a well-greased 9-inch pie plate to form an even crust.

In a small mixing bowl combine 1 egg, cottage cheese, and pepper. Spread over the spaghetti crust; set aside.

In a large skillet cook the sausage, mushrooms, onion, and green pepper till the meat is brown and vegetables are tender. Drain fat. Stir in pizza sauce. Cook till heated through. Spoon meat mixture over cottage cheese mixture. Cover loosely with foil.

Bake in a 350° oven for 20 minutes. Remove foil; sprinkle with mozzarella cheese. Bake, uncovered, about 5 minutes more or till mozzarella cheese melts. Let stand 5 minutes before serving. Cut into wedges to serve. Makes 4 or 5 servings.

Nutrition information per serving: 442 calories, 30 g protein, 39 g carbohydrate, 18 g fat (6 g saturated), 155 mg cholesterol, 848 mg sodium.

Polish Sausage and Spaghetti in Beer

Sausage, caraway seed, and beer add up to a pasta dish with a German twist.

1   pound fully cooked Polish sausage
      or smoked sausage, cut into
      1-inch pieces
1   cup sliced fresh mushrooms
2   stalks celery, sliced (1 cup)
1   large green sweet pepper, cut into
      1-inch pieces
1   medium onion, chopped (½ cup)
1   cup beer
1   8-ounce can tomato sauce
½   cup water
2   tablespoons snipped parsley
½   teaspoon sugar
½   teaspoon caraway seed
4   ounces packaged dried spaghetti,
      broken into 2-inch pieces
      Grated Parmesan cheese (optional)

In a Dutch oven or large saucepan cook the sausage till light brown. Remove sausage; set aside.

Add mushrooms, celery, green pepper, and onion to Dutch oven. Cook and stir about 3 minutes or till vegetables are tender. Drain fat. Stir in beer, tomato sauce, water, parsley, sugar, and caraway seed. Bring to boiling; reduce heat. Cover and simmer for 20 minutes. Stir in spaghetti.

Return to boiling; reduce heat. Cover and simmer for 10 to 12 minutes more or till spaghetti is tender. Add sausage; heat through. Serve in bowls and, if desired, pass Parmesan cheese. Makes 4 servings.

Nutrition information per serving: 549 calories, 22 g protein, 36 g carbohydrate, 33 g fat (12 g saturated), 79 mg cholesterol, 1,370 mg sodium.

Ham, Spinach, and Mostaccioli Casserole

Just before serving, be sure to give the casserole a good stir to distribute the rich and creamy sauce.

8   ounces packaged dried mostaccioli,
      cut ziti, or elbow macaroni
3   tablespoons margarine or butter
3   medium onions, cut into thin
      wedges, or 5 medium leeks, sliced
2   cloves garlic, minced
¼   cup all-purpose flour
½   teaspoon dried thyme, crushed
⅛   teaspoon pepper
1½ cups half-and-half, light cream,
      or milk
1½ cups chicken broth
1½ cups cubed fully cooked ham
1   10-ounce package frozen chopped
      spinach, thawed and drained

Cook pasta according to package directions. Drain pasta; rinse with cold water. Drain again.

In a large saucepan melt margarine or butter. Add onions or leeks and garlic. Cover and cook about 5 minutes or till onions are tender; stir occasionally. Stir in flour, thyme, and pepper. Add half-and-half, light cream, or milk and the chicken broth all at once. Cook and stir till thickened and bubbly. Cook and stir for 1 minute more. Stir in pasta, ham, and spinach. Spoon mixture into a 3-quart casserole.

Cover and bake in a 350° oven for 30 to 35 minutes or till heated through. Let stand 5 minutes. Stir gently before serving. Makes 6 servings.

Nutrition information per serving: 388 calories, 18 g protein, 44 g carbohydrate, 16 g fat (6 g saturated), 42 mg cholesterol, 719 mg sodium.

Thawing Spinach

When you forget to thaw frozen spinach ahead of time, place the unwrapped frozen block of spinach in a colander and run hot water over it, breaking up the block with a fork. If you prefer, you can micro-thaw spinach by placing the unwrapped block in a bowl and micro-cooking it on 30% power (medium-low) for 2 to 4 minutes or until soft enough to break into chunks. Continue to cook the spinach on 30% power for 3 to 5 minutes or until thawed.

Swiss Chicken Bundles

This tarragon-scented lasagna makes an elegant dish for a bridal or baby shower.

8 packaged dried lasagna noodles
1 beaten egg
2 cups ricotta cheese or cream-style
   cottage cheese, drained
1½ cups chopped cooked chicken
   (8 ounces)
1½ teaspoons snipped fresh tarragon or
   basil or ¼ teaspoon dried tarragon
   or basil, crushed
2 tablespoons margarine or butter
2 tablespoons all-purpose flour
½ teaspoon dry mustard
¼ teaspoon salt
⅛ teaspoon pepper
1½ cups milk
1½ cups shredded process Swiss cheese
   (6 ounces)
   Paprika or snipped parsley
   (optional)
   Fresh tarragon sprigs (optional)

Cook lasagna noodles according to package directions. Drain noodles; rinse with cold water. Drain again.

For filling, in a medium mixing bowl stir together egg, ricotta or cottage cheese, chicken, and 1½ teaspoons tarragon or basil.

To assemble bundles, spread about ⅓ cup of the filling over each lasagna noodle. Roll up noodles, starting from a short end. Place bundles, seam sides down, in a 2-quart rectangular baking dish; set aside.

For sauce, in a medium saucepan melt the margarine or butter. Stir in flour, mustard, salt, and pepper. Add milk all at once. Cook and stir till thickened and bubbly. Gradually add cheese, stirring till melted after each addition. Pour sauce over lasagna bundles. Cover dish with foil.

Bake in a 375° oven for 30 to 35 minutes or till heated through. Let stand 10 minutes before serving. Transfer bundles to individual plates. Stir sauce in baking dish. Spoon some of the sauce over each bundle and, if desired, sprinkle with paprika or parsley. If desired, garnish with fresh tarragon sprigs. Makes 8 servings.

Nutrition information per serving: 347 calories, 25 g protein, 22 g carbohydrate, 17 g fat (8 g saturated), 92 mg cholesterol, 523 mg sodium.

Saucy Chicken Rigatoni

While cooking this saucepan dinner, stir every now and then to prevent the pasta from sticking to the pan.

1   medium onion, chopped (½ cup)
1   clove garlic, minced
1   tablespoon cooking oil
1   14½-ounce can tomatoes, cut up
1   7½-ounce can tomatoes, cut up
2   cups packaged dried rigatoni or
      elbow macaroni
1¼ cups water
1   2½-ounce jar sliced mushrooms,
      drained
1   teaspoon dried Italian seasoning,
      crushed
⅛   teaspoon ground red pepper
      (optional)
1½ cups chopped cooked chicken or
      turkey (8 ounces)
    Fresh basil leaves (optional)

In a large saucepan cook onion and garlic in hot oil till tender. Stir in both cans of undrained tomatoes, pasta, water, mushrooms, Italian seasoning, and, if desired, ground red pepper. Bring to boiling; reduce heat. Cover and simmer about 20 minutes or till pasta is tender but slightly firm, stirring occasionally.

Stir in chicken or turkey; heat through. If desired, garnish with fresh basil leaves. Makes 4 servings.

Nutrition information per serving: 293 calories, 22 g protein, 32 g carbohydrate, 9 g fat (2 g saturated), 51 mg cholesterol, 399 mg sodium.

Pasta with Chicken and Pepper-Cheese Sauce

Ground red, white, and black and jalapeño peppers multiply the hotness by four in this zippy cream sauce.

8 ounces packaged dried spaghetti or fettuccine

3 small skinless, boneless chicken breast halves (about 8 ounces total)

1 tablespoon all-purpose flour

½ teaspoon salt

¼ to ½ teaspoon ground red pepper

⅛ to ¼ teaspoon ground white pepper

⅛ to ¼ teaspoon ground black pepper

1 tablespoon cooking oil

1 medium red or green sweet pepper, chopped (1 cup)

1 medium onion, chopped (½ cup)

1 tablespoon chopped, seeded jalapeño pepper

2 cloves garlic, minced

2 tablespoons all-purpose flour

¾ cup chicken broth

½ cup milk

1 teaspoon Worcestershire sauce

1 cup shredded Monterey Jack or cheddar cheese (4 ounces)

¼ cup dairy sour cream

1 jalapeño pepper, thinly sliced (optional)

Cook pasta according to package directions. Drain; keep warm.

Rinse chicken; pat dry with paper towels. Cut into 1-inch pieces. In a small mixing bowl combine the 1 tablespoon flour, salt, red pepper, white pepper, and black pepper. Toss flour mixture with chicken to coat. Set aside.

In a large skillet heat the oil over medium-high heat. (Add more oil as necessary during cooking.) Add sweet pepper, onion, chopped jalapeño pepper, and garlic; cook and stir till vegetables are tender. Remove the vegetables with a slotted spoon; set aside.

Add chicken to the skillet. Cook and stir for 4 to 5 minutes or till chicken is tender and no longer pink. Remove chicken from skillet.

Stir 2 tablespoons flour into drippings in skillet. Add chicken broth, milk, and Worcestershire sauce. Cook and stir till thickened and bubbly. Add the Monterey Jack or cheddar cheese, stirring till cheese melts. Stir 1 cup of the hot mixture into the sour cream; return all of the sour cream mixture to skillet. Stir in chicken and vegetables. Cook till heated through. Do not boil.

Arrange pasta on individual plates or a large platter. Spoon the chicken mixture over pasta. If desired, garnish with jalapeño pepper slices. Makes 4 servings.

Nutrition information per serving: 512 calories, 29 g protein, 56 g carbohydrate, 19 g fat (9 g saturated), 64 mg cholesterol, 660 mg sodium.

Chicken Manicotti with Chive Cream Sauce

Broccoli and pimiento add vivid colors to the tasty chicken filling that spills from these pasta shells.

12 packaged dried manicotti shells
1 8-ounce container soft-style cream
    cheese with chives and onion
⅔ cup milk
¼ cup grated Romano or Parmesan
    cheese
2 cups chopped cooked chicken
    (10 ounces)
1 10-ounce package frozen chopped
    broccoli, thawed and drained
½ of a 7-ounce jar roasted red
    sweet peppers, drained and sliced,
    or one 4-ounce jar diced
    pimiento, drained
¼ teaspoon black pepper
    Paprika

Cook manicotti shells according to package directions. Drain shells; rinse with cold water. Drain again.

Meanwhile, for sauce, in a small heavy saucepan melt cream cheese over medium-low heat; stir constantly. Slowly add milk, stirring till smooth. Stir in Romano or Parmesan cheese. Remove from heat.

For filling, in a medium mixing bowl stir together ¾ cup of the sauce, chicken, broccoli, roasted red sweet peppers or pimiento, and black pepper. Using a small spoon, carefully fill each manicotti shell with about ⅓ cup of the filling.

Arrange the filled shells in a 3-quart rectangular baking dish. Pour the remaining sauce over the shells. Sprinkle with paprika. Cover with foil.

Bake in a 350° oven for 25 to 30 minutes or till heated through. Makes 6 servings.

Nutrition information per serving: 396 calories, 25 g protein, 31 g carbohydrate, 18 g fat (9 g saturated), 92 mg cholesterol, 257 mg sodium.

Linguine with Chicken and Peanut Sauce

This garlic- and ginger-scented chicken dinner offers a taste of the Orient.

8 ounces packaged dried linguine or
   spaghetti
1 14½-ounce can chicken broth
2 tablespoons dry white wine or water
2 tablespoons soy sauce
1 tablespoon cornstarch
⅛ to ¼ teaspoon ground red pepper
½ cup peanut butter
4 medium skinless, boneless chicken
   breast halves (about 12 ounces
   total)
1 tablespoon cooking oil
1 medium onion, halved lengthwise
   and thinly sliced
2 cloves garlic, minced
1 teaspoon grated gingerroot
2 green onions, sliced (¼ cup)
   Orange slices, cut in half (optional)
   Grapes (optional)

Cook pasta according to package directions. Drain; keep warm.

For sauce, in a medium mixing bowl stir together chicken broth, wine or water, soy sauce, cornstarch, and red pepper. Stir in peanut butter till smooth. Rinse chicken; pat dry with paper towels. Cut into 1-inch pieces. Set aside.

In a wok or large skillet heat the cooking oil over medium-high heat. (Add more oil as necessary during cooking.) Add onion, garlic, and gingerroot to hot oil; stir-fry for 2 to 3 minutes or till onion is crisp-tender. Remove onion mixture from wok.

Add the chicken to the wok. Stir-fry about 3 minutes or till chicken is tender and no longer pink. Push the chicken from the center of the wok. Stir sauce; add to center of the wok. Cook and stir till thickened and bubbly. Cook and stir for 2 minutes more. Return onion mixture to wok; stir all ingredients together.

Arrange pasta on individual plates or a large platter. Spoon the chicken mixture over pasta. Sprinkle with green onions. If desired, garnish with orange slices and grapes. Makes 4 servings.

Nutrition information per serving: 579 calories, 35 g protein, 57 g carbohydrate, 23 g fat (5 g saturated), 45 mg cholesterol, 1,038 mg sodium.

Turkey Lasagna Rolls

For this robust lasagna-style entrée, roll the noodles around a cheesy spinach filling and then top them with a turkey and tomato sauce.

8   ounces ground raw turkey
1   medium onion, chopped (½ cup)
2   cloves garlic, minced
1   cup sliced fresh mushrooms
1   cup water
1   7½-ounce can tomatoes, cut up
1   6-ounce can tomato paste
1½ teaspoons dried oregano, crushed
1   teaspoon dried basil, crushed
8   packaged dried lasagna noodles
1   beaten egg
1   15-ounce carton ricotta cheese
1   10-ounce package frozen chopped
     spinach, thawed and drained
1½ cups shredded mozzarella cheese
     (6 ounces)
1   cup grated Parmesan cheese
     Fresh parsley sprigs (optional)

For sauce, in a large skillet cook turkey, onion, and garlic till turkey is no longer pink; drain fat. Stir in mushrooms, water, undrained tomatoes, tomato paste, oregano, and basil. Bring to boiling; reduce heat. Cover and simmer for 25 minutes.

Meanwhile, cook the lasagna noodles according to package directions. Drain noodles; rinse with cold water. Drain again.

For filling, in a mixing bowl stir together egg, ricotta cheese, spinach, 1 cup of the mozzarella cheese, and ¾ cup of the Parmesan cheese.

To assemble rolls, spread about ½ cup of the filling over each lasagna noodle. Roll up noodles, starting from a short end. Place lasagna rolls, seam sides down, in a 2-quart rectangular baking dish. Pour sauce over lasagna rolls. Cover dish with foil.

Bake in a 375° oven for 25 minutes. Remove foil. Sprinkle with remaining mozzarella cheese. Bake for 5 to 10 minutes more or till heated through. Let stand 5 minutes before serving. Sprinkle with remaining Parmesan cheese and, if desired, garnish with parsley sprigs. Makes 8 servings.

Nutrition information per serving: 345 calories, 26 g protein, 28 g carbohydrate, 15 g fat (8 g saturated), 75 mg cholesterol, 511 mg sodium.

Turkey and Fruit Pasta Salad

Savor this refreshing honey-dressed salad in the summertime when nectarines are at their peak.

1	cup packaged dried rope macaroni (gemelli) or 1⅓ cups corkscrew macaroni (4 ounces)
1½	cups chopped cooked turkey or chicken or fully cooked turkey ham (8 ounces)
2	green onions, sliced (¼ cup)
⅓	cup lime or lemon juice
¼	cup salad oil
1	tablespoon honey
2	teaspoons snipped fresh thyme or ½ teaspoon dried thyme, crushed
2	medium nectarines or plums, sliced
1	cup halved fresh strawberries

Cook pasta according to package directions. Drain pasta; rinse with cold water. Drain again.

In a large mixing bowl combine pasta; turkey, chicken, or turkey ham; and green onions. Toss to mix.

For dressing, in a screw-top jar combine lime or lemon juice, oil, honey, and thyme. Cover and shake well. Pour dressing over pasta mixture; toss to coat. Cover and chill for 4 to 24 hours.

Just before serving, add the nectarines or plums and strawberries. Toss to mix. Makes 4 servings.

Nutrition information per serving: 393 calories, 21 g protein, 39 g carbohydrate, 17 g fat (3 g saturated), 43 mg cholesterol, 42 mg sodium.

Pasta for Salads

The secret to fresh-tasting pasta salads is to avoid overcooking. Pasta cooked to just the right stage is called *al dente*, which means "to the tooth" in Italian. At this point, the pasta has a firm texture and is slightly chewy.

Spaghetti with Turkey Meatballs

We updated everyone's favorite pasta dish by using ground turkey instead of ground beef.

1   large onion, chopped (1 cup)
1   medium green sweet pepper,
      coarsely chopped (1 cup)
1   medium carrot, coarsely chopped
      (½ cup)
1   stalk celery, sliced (½ cup)
1   tablespoon cooking oil
4   large ripe tomatoes, peeled and
      chopped (4 cups), or two
      14½-ounce cans tomatoes, cut up
1   6-ounce can (⅔ cup) tomato paste
2   teaspoons dried Italian seasoning,
      crushed
½   teaspoon sugar
½   teaspoon salt
½   teaspoon garlic powder
    Turkey Meatballs
12 ounces packaged dried spaghetti or
      mostaccioli

For sauce, in a Dutch oven cook onion, green pepper, carrot, and celery in hot oil till tender. Stir in fresh or undrained canned tomatoes, tomato paste, Italian seasoning, sugar, salt, and garlic powder. Bring to boiling. Add Turkey Meatballs; reduce heat. Cover and simmer for 30 minutes. If necessary, uncover and simmer for 10 to 15 minutes more or till sauce is desired consistency, stirring occasionally.

Meanwhile, cook the pasta according to package directions. Drain.

Arrange pasta on individual plates or a large platter. Spoon the meatballs and sauce over pasta. Makes 6 servings.

Turkey Meatballs: In a medium mixing bowl combine 1 beaten *egg;* 2 tablespoons *milk;* ¼ cup *fine dry bread crumbs;* ½ teaspoon *salt;* ½ teaspoon *dried Italian seasoning,* crushed; and ½ teaspoon *pepper.* Add 1 pound *ground raw turkey;* mix well. With wet hands, shape mixture into twenty-four 1-inch meatballs. Place the meatballs in a greased 13x9x2-inch baking pan. Bake in a 375° oven about 20 minutes or till turkey is no longer pink. Drain fat.

Nutrition information per serving: 442 calories, 22 g protein, 65 g carbohydrate, 11 g fat (2 g saturated), 64 mg cholesterol, 686 mg sodium.

Creamy Seafood Lasagna

Tender morsels of seafood in a sour cream sauce take lasagna to new heights.

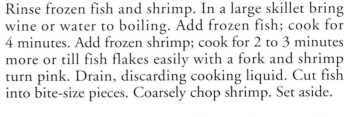

1   12-ounce package frozen fish fillets
1   8-ounce package frozen, peeled, deveined shrimp
1½ cups dry white wine or water
6   packaged dried lasagna noodles
1   beaten egg
2   cups ricotta cheese or cream-style cottage cheese, drained
½   cup grated Parmesan cheese
4   teaspoons snipped fresh basil or 1 teaspoon dried basil, crushed
1   cup sliced fresh mushrooms
2   green onions, sliced (¼ cup)
3   tablespoons margarine or butter
3   tablespoons all-purpose flour
¼   teaspoon salt
¼   teaspoon ground white pepper
1⅓ cups milk
½   cup dairy sour cream
1   8-ounce package sliced mozzarella cheese

Rinse frozen fish and shrimp. In a large skillet bring wine or water to boiling. Add frozen fish; cook for 4 minutes. Add frozen shrimp; cook for 2 to 3 minutes more or till fish flakes easily with a fork and shrimp turn pink. Drain, discarding cooking liquid. Cut fish into bite-size pieces. Coarsely chop shrimp. Set aside.

Meanwhile, cook lasagna noodles according to package directions. Drain; rinse with cold water. Drain again.

For filling, in a small mixing bowl combine egg, ricotta or cottage cheese, half of the Parmesan cheese, and the basil. Set filling aside.

For sauce, in a medium saucepan cook mushrooms and green onions in margarine or butter till tender. Stir in flour, salt, and pepper. Add milk all at once. Cook and stir till thickened and bubbly. Remove from heat. Stir about 1 cup of the hot mixture into the sour cream; return all of the sour cream mixture to the saucepan. Stir fish and shrimp into the sauce.

To assemble, layer half of the cooked noodles in a 2-quart rectangular baking dish. Spread with half of the filling. Top with half of the sauce and half of the mozzarella cheese. Repeat layers. Sprinkle with the remaining Parmesan cheese.

Bake in a 375° oven for 30 to 35 minutes or till heated through. Let stand 10 minutes before serving. Makes 10 servings.

Nutrition information per serving: *336 calories, 28 g protein, 16 g carbohydrate, 17 g fat (9 g saturated), 106 mg cholesterol, 441 mg sodium.*

Fish and Shell Stew

To vary the flavor, try switching to Cajun-style or Mexican-style stewed tomatoes.

12	ounces fresh or frozen skinless fish fillets (cod, pike, or orange roughy)
2	14½-ounce cans chicken broth
1	15-ounce can garbanzo beans or red kidney beans, rinsed and drained
1	cup loose-pack frozen mixed vegetables
¾	cup packaged dried medium shell macaroni or cavatelli
1	medium onion, chopped (½ cup)
1	teaspoon dried basil or thyme, crushed
¼	teaspoon pepper
1	14½-ounce can Italian-style stewed tomatoes

Thaw fish, if frozen. Rinse fish. Cut into 1-inch pieces; set aside.

In a large saucepan stir together broth, beans, frozen vegetables, pasta, onion, basil or thyme, and pepper. Bring to boiling; reduce heat. Cover and simmer for 10 minutes.

Stir in undrained tomatoes and fish. Return to boiling; reduce heat. Cover and simmer for 2 to 3 minutes or till fish flakes easily with a fork. Makes 4 servings.

Nutrition information per serving: 291 calories, 26 g protein, 39 g carbohydrate, 4 g fat (1 g saturated), 34 mg cholesterol, 1,261 mg sodium.

Linguine with Salmon

If you are using the smoked salmon, omit the salt when cooking the pasta. You'll find the smoked salmon adds all the saltiness you need.

8 ounces packaged dried linguine, fettuccine, or spaghetti
6 ounces cooked fresh salmon or thinly sliced, smoked salmon (lox-style)
2 green onions, thinly sliced (¼ cup)
1 clove garlic, minced
1 tablespoon margarine or butter
1 cup whipping cream
1 tablespoon snipped fresh dill or 1 teaspoon dried dillweed
1 teaspoon finely shredded lemon peel
¼ teaspoon pepper
2 tablespoons grated Parmesan cheese
Fresh dill sprigs (optional)
Lemon wedges (optional)

Cook pasta according to package directions. Drain; keep warm.

Meanwhile, break the fresh salmon into chunks or cut the smoked salmon into thin bite-size strips; set aside.

For sauce, in a large skillet cook the green onions and garlic in margarine or butter till tender. Stir in the whipping cream, snipped fresh or dried dillweed, lemon peel, and pepper. Bring to boiling; reduce heat. Boil gently about 5 minutes or till slightly thickened. Stir in fresh or smoked salmon; heat through. Remove from heat. Gently stir in Parmesan cheese.

Arrange pasta on individual plates or a large platter. Spoon the sauce over the pasta. If desired, garnish with fresh dill sprigs and lemon wedges. Makes 4 servings.

Nutrition information per serving: 523 calories, 18 g protein, 48 g carbohydrate, 29 g fat (15 g saturated), 94 mg cholesterol, 450 mg sodium.

Fettuccine with Herbed Shrimp

A white wine and herb sauce dresses the shrimp and pasta in this elegant entrée.

12	ounces fresh or frozen, peeled, deveined shrimp
6	ounces packaged dried plain and/or spinach fettuccine
2	cups sliced fresh mushrooms
1	large onion, chopped (1 cup)
2	cloves garlic, minced
1	tablespoon olive oil or cooking oil
¼	cup dry white wine
1	tablespoon instant chicken bouillon granules
1	tablespoon snipped fresh basil or 1 teaspoon dried basil, crushed
1½	teaspoons snipped fresh oregano or ½ teaspoon dried oregano, crushed
1	teaspoon cornstarch
⅛	teaspoon pepper
2	medium tomatoes, peeled, seeded, and chopped
¼	cup grated Parmesan cheese
¼	cup snipped parsley

Thaw shrimp, if frozen. Rinse shrimp; pat dry with paper towels. Cut shrimp in half lengthwise; set aside.

Cook pasta according to package directions. Drain; keep warm.

Meanwhile, in a large saucepan cook mushrooms, onion, and garlic in hot oil till onion is tender.

In a small mixing bowl stir together wine, bouillon granules, basil, oregano, cornstarch, and pepper. Add to mushroom mixture. Cook and stir till thickened and bubbly.

Add shrimp to mushroom mixture. Cover and simmer about 2 minutes or till shrimp turn pink. Stir in the tomatoes; heat through.

Spoon the shrimp mixture over pasta. Sprinkle with Parmesan cheese and parsley. Toss to coat. Makes 4 servings.

Nutrition information per serving: 351 calories, 25 g protein, 44 g carbohydrate, 7 g fat (2 g saturated), 136 mg cholesterol, 926 mg sodium.

Roasted Red Pepper Sauce Over Tortellini

For leisurely dining, start in the fast lane. Take advantage of ready-to-use roasted peppers and tortellini to speed up meal preparation. Then, slow down and enjoy the delectable result.

1   9-ounce package refrigerated
      meat- or cheese-filled tortellini
1   12-ounce jar roasted red sweet
      peppers, drained
½   cup chopped onion
3   cloves garlic, minced
1   tablespoon margarine or butter
2   teaspoons snipped fresh thyme or
      ½ teaspoon dried thyme, crushed
2   teaspoons snipped fresh oregano or
      ¼ teaspoon dried oregano,
      crushed
1   teaspoon sugar

Cook tortellini according to package directions. Drain; keep warm.

Meanwhile, place roasted sweet peppers in a food processor bowl or blender container. Cover and process or blend till smooth. Set aside.

For sauce, in a medium saucepan cook the onion and garlic in margarine or butter till tender. Add pureed roasted peppers, thyme, oregano, and sugar. Cook and stir till heated through.

Pour the sauce over the tortellini. Toss to coat. Makes 3 servings.

Nutrition information per serving: 343 calories, 14 g protein, 40 g carbohydrate, 15 g fat (4 g saturated), 75 mg cholesterol, 298 mg sodium.

Pasta Primavera

A great dish to celebrate summertime and garden-fresh vegetables.

8 ounces fresh wax or green beans, cut
    into 2-inch pieces (2 cups)
8 ounces fresh asparagus, cut into
    2-inch pieces (1½ cups)
1 cup broccoli flowerets
8 ounces packaged dried vermicelli or
    spaghetti
½ of a medium red or green sweet
    pepper, cut into 1-inch pieces
2 green onions, sliced (¼ cup)
1 tablespoon margarine or butter
1¼ cups chicken broth
    Dash ground nutmeg
1 8-ounce carton plain low-fat yogurt
3 tablespoons all-purpose flour
½ cup grated Parmesan cheese
½ cup pine nuts or slivered almonds,
    toasted

In a large saucepan cook beans in a small amount of boiling salted water for 15 minutes. Add asparagus and broccoli. Cook for 5 to 10 minutes more or till the vegetables are crisp-tender. Drain; keep warm.

Meanwhile, cook the pasta according to package directions. Drain; keep warm.

For sauce, cook the sweet pepper and green onions in margarine or butter till tender. Stir in chicken broth and nutmeg. Bring to boiling; reduce heat. Stir together yogurt and flour; add to broth mixture. Cook and stir till thickened and bubbly. Stir in Parmesan cheese. Cook and stir about 1 minute more or till smooth. Pour over cooked vegetables; toss to coat.

Arrange pasta on individual plates or a large platter. Spoon the sauce over the pasta. Sprinkle with pine nuts or almonds. Makes 4 servings.

Nutrition information per serving: 510 calories, 25 g protein, 64 g carbohydrate, 20 g fat (5 g saturated), 13 mg cholesterol, 557 mg sodium.

Pasta Rosa-Verde

This red, white, and green dish on the table will make any flag-waving Italian feel patriotic (not to mention famished)! Fresh tomatoes are quick-cooked with peppery arugula and topped with tangy Gorgonzola cheese. (Also pictured on the cover.)

8	ounces packaged dried cut ziti or mostaccioli
1	medium onion, thinly sliced
2	cloves garlic, minced
1	tablespoon olive oil
4	to 6 medium tomatoes, seeded and coarsely chopped
1	teaspoon salt
½	teaspoon freshly ground black pepper
¼	teaspoon crushed red pepper (optional)
3	cups arugula, watercress, and/or spinach, coarsely chopped
¼	cup pine nuts or slivered almonds, toasted
2	tablespoons crumbled Gorgonzola or other blue cheese

Cook pasta according to package directions. Drain; keep warm.

Meanwhile, for sauce, in a large skillet cook the onion and garlic in hot olive oil over medium heat till onion is tender.

Add tomatoes, salt, black pepper, and, if desired, red pepper. Cook and stir over medium-high heat about 2 minutes or till the tomatoes are warm and release some of their juices. Stir in arugula, watercress, and/or spinach. Heat just till greens are wilted.

Arrange the pasta in individual serving bowls. Spoon the sauce over the pasta. Sprinkle with toasted pine nuts or almonds and Gorgonzola or other blue cheese. Makes 4 servings.

Nutrition information per serving: 352 calories, 12 g protein, 54 g carbohydrate, 11 g fat (2 g saturated), 3 mg cholesterol, 610 mg sodium.

Tortellini with Vegetable Sauce

Prefer ravioli? Serve the fresh vegetable sauce over a 9-ounce package of refrigerated ravioli.

1 medium onion, chopped (½ cup)
1 stalk celery, sliced (½ cup)
2 cloves garlic, minced
1 tablespoon margarine or butter
2 pounds ripe tomatoes, peeled and chopped (3 cups), or one 28-ounce can tomatoes, cut up
1 cup sliced fresh mushrooms
½ cup chopped green sweet pepper
1 tablespoon snipped fresh sage or 1 teaspoon dried sage, crushed
½ teaspoon sugar
¼ teaspoon salt
⅛ teaspoon pepper
1 small yellow summer squash or zucchini, cut into ½-inch pieces
1 8-ounce package dried tortellini or one 9-ounce package refrigerated tortellini

For sauce, in a large saucepan cook onion, celery, and garlic in margarine or butter till tender. Stir in fresh or undrained canned tomatoes, mushrooms, green pepper, sage, sugar, salt, and pepper. Bring to boiling; reduce heat. Simmer, uncovered, for 40 minutes.

Stir summer squash or zucchini into tomato mixture. Cook about 5 minutes more or till sauce is desired consistency and squash is tender.

Meanwhile, cook the tortellini according to package directions. Drain. Toss tortellini with sauce. Makes 4 servings.

Nutrition information per serving: 295 calories, 14 g protein, 48 g carbohydrate, 7 g fat (1g saturated), 35 mg cholesterol, 484 mg sodium.

Pasta Twists with Beer-Cheese Sauce

Be sure to use sharp cheddar for the cheesiest flavor.

8 ounces packaged dried tri-colored corkscrew macaroni or rope macaroni (gemelli)
2 medium carrots, bias-sliced (1 cup)
1 small zucchini, coarsely chopped (1 cup)
1 cup fresh whole mushrooms, quartered
2 tablespoons margarine or butter
2 tablespoons all-purpose flour
1 cup milk
¼ cup beer
¾ cup shredded sharp cheddar cheese (3 ounces)

Cook pasta according to package directions. Drain; keep warm.

Meanwhile, for sauce, in a medium saucepan cook carrots, zucchini, and mushrooms in margarine or butter till tender. Stir in flour. Add milk all at once. Cook and stir over medium heat till thickened and bubbly. Cook and stir for 1 minute more. Add beer and heat through. Remove from heat. Gradually add cheddar cheese, stirring just till melted. If desired, season to taste with salt and pepper.

Arrange pasta on individual plates or a large platter. Spoon the sauce over pasta. Makes 4 servings.

Nutrition information per serving: 426 calories, 16 g protein, 55 g carbohydrate, 15 g fat (6 g saturated), 27 mg cholesterol, 253 mg sodium.

INDEX